The Blessed God
by Daniel Burgess
with chapters by C. Matthew McMahon

Copyright Information

The Blessed God by Daniel Burgess, with chapters by C. Matthew McMahon
Edited by Therese B. McMahon and Susan Ruth

Copyright © 2021 by Puritan Publications and A Puritan's Mind®

Some language has been updated from the original manuscript. Any change in wording or punctuation has not changed the intent or meaning of the original author(s), and has been made to aid the modern reader.

Published by Puritan Publications
A Ministry of A Puritan's Mind® in Crossville, TN
www.apuritansmind.com
www.puritanpublications.com

All rights reserved. No part of this publication may be reproduced, stored in a retrieval system or transmitted in any form by any means, electronic, mechanical, photocopy, recording or otherwise, without the prior permission of the publisher, except as provided by USA copyright law.

This Print Edition, 2021
Electronic Edition, 2021
Manufactured in the United States of America

ISBN: 978-1-62663-393-3
eISBN: 978-1-62663-392-6

Table of Contents

God Can Be Known 4

Meet Daniel Burgess 10

To the Congregation Under My Care....................................16

Part 1: Truths About God 18

Part 2: Truths Necessary for Salvation 29

Part 3: Truths on Assurance of Salvation........................... 49

Postscript..68

Other Helpful Works from Daniel Burgess at Puritan Publications 71

God Can Be Known
by C. Matthew McMahon, Ph.D., Th.D.

The Bible teaches that God *can* be known. Is this a strange statement to make? To have a God that is unlike the creature, a God who is infinite in all respects, high and lofty and lifted up, does not beg the question, but presses it to our hearts and minds to consider. If God is high and lofty, if he is altogether "other," or incomprehensible and imperceptible, can he actually be known? What if we say it this way, that men and angels can never comprehend that perfection which dwells in God; for the perfection of God is unsearchable, and therefore, incomprehensible. Can something *incomprehensible* be known? That is somewhat of a tricky question to answer.

Let's consider, briefly, another statement, that the Bible teaches that eternal life *consists* in the knowledge of God and of Jesus Christ, his one and only Son. In Christ's high priestly prayer, he said this about *defining* eternal life, "And this is life eternal, that they might *know* thee the only true God, and Jesus Christ, whom thou hast sent," (John 17:3). What do we make of this? If the Bible teaches that knowledge of God is eternal life, knowledge of God and his Son, and God is *incomprehensible*, what does the Christian do in rectifying this dilemma?

Consider a couple of verses in God's word. Psalm 76:1 states, "In Judah *is God known*: his name is great in Israel." Isaiah 11:9 states, "They shall not hurt nor destroy in all my holy mountain: for the earth shall be *full of the knowledge of the LORD, as the waters cover the sea.*" The Apostle Peter quotes this in 2 Peter 3:18, "They shall not hurt nor destroy in all my holy mountain: for the earth shall be full of the knowledge of the LORD, as the waters cover the sea." Has Peter got it all wrong? Did he misunderstand Jesus, and the Old Testament? Contrary to playing devil's advocate, Scriptures like these are *very comforting.* They tell us that God exists, and that he *can* be known. This does not mean that Christians can know *all that is true* concerning God. Finite creatures cannot, "comprehend God," (know him completely and fully), rather, we, "apprehend," God, (understand him in part as to what *he has revealed* to us about himself in his word).

    In communicating truth to the reader in the Bible, human beings form ideas about God based on what they understand and learn from propositional truth; and if they think God's thoughts after him, and if they do that in the *responsible* way, with the right application of that knowledge to their heart, they come to *know God* intimately. How much one knows or does not know *about Scripture* dictates what they know or not know *about God.* That is a very simple principle that Christian's often forget: what one knows *about God's revealed word about himself in Scripture,* dictates how much one will know God, and how much one knows God will dictate how one will *serve this God.* The ramifications of this are almost endless to consider. When the Bible *defines* God, what that means is that humans are able to formulate an idea of God as it lies in their mind represented by the truth of his word. He reveals truth in a way that humans can understand it. This in turn gives them a certain amount of cognizance about who God is, and what God has done in both creating the universe, and saving his people. In this, *truth matters*.

Christians are often confused with the question, "Can God be known?" because they immediately assume that we mean, "Can God be fully and perfectly known, and is being fully and perfectly known necessary for salvation?" To know God and Jesus Christ whom he has sent, is to know both God and Jesus Christ in a *limited* sense. Would it not be very odd that human beings could find out God to perfection?[1] God is *past* finding out. He is infinite, and they are finite. How could a finite being contain infinite knowledge, and that perfectly? No, they cannot understand "the Almighty unto perfection." In fact, human beings do not know the deep essence as well as the attributes of *any singular thing to perfection*, much less the incomprehensible God. That kind of knowledge is only something God possesses. But what *can* they know?

People are able to know both what creation teaches them about God, as well as the book of special revelation in God's word. They can know all kinds of things based on those two sources. Nature teaches them about God (his invisible attributes and divine qualities), *and* God

---

[1] See Job 5:9, 9:10 and Rom. 11:33 as samples of this question posed in Scripture. Zophar asks this question rhetorically, "Canst thou by searching find out God? canst thou find out the Almighty unto perfection?" (Job. 11:7). The answer is a resounding *no*.

specifically teaches them about himself in his word. And what they know, and what they come to learn, is eminently reliable if they rest on the revelation of God to direct them, and the Spirit of God to spiritually persuade them of the truth. How will the Christian answer Isaiah, "To whom then will ye liken God? or what likeness will ye compare unto Him?" (Isa. 40:1). And yet, at the same time, King Jesus says, "And this is life eternal, *that they might know thee* the only true God, and Jesus Christ, whom thou hast sent," (John 17:3). Christians rejoice in the fact that, "the Son of God is come, and hath given us an understanding, that we *know* him that is true, and we are in him that is true, even in his Son Jesus Christ," (1 John 5:20). Yes, God is in his essence, incomprehensible, and yet in his revelation to his people, he is *knowable*. They can catch glimpses of his divine glory as he reveals them clearly in his word.

To *know God* is what Daniel Burgess teaches in this work. It is not only to know God as God has revealed his essence, but Burgess, as all good, practical preachers do, presses the reader to then take what they learn about God, and see how it necessarily links to truths necessary for salvation; in other words, what does the knowledge of God and Christ do for the believer? And then, after joining those two concepts together, he shows how one may be truly *assured* of their salvation based on these truths. In this, Burgess covers three important questions. Question 1: What conceptions should we have of the blessed God? Question 2: What are those truths of the knowledge of God which appear indispensably necessary and spiritually desirable to our salvation? Question 3: What is that change brought about in a man by God's holy word and Spirit, before he can safely conclude himself to be passed from death to life? These are, most assuredly, three of the most important questions that can be drawn from Scripture and applied to the life of any fallen son of Adam.

In showing these as *utterly* important as they refer to eternal realities, Burgess not only explains *who* God is, but also the *work* that God has done in Jesus Christ who is the perfect God and perfect man in one person to overcome the horrible effects of a fallen world. To know salvation, is to know, first, who God is, and *then* what he does in and through his Christ. He will explain who this Jesus is as the great Prophet, Priest and King in both his states of humiliation and exaltation; that in Christ's humiliation he was made under the law, obeying the precepts, and suffering its curse. And in his exaltation, in rising from the dead as he did, ascending into heaven, and having all power in heaven and earth given him, he is made higher than any mere creature could possibly be exalted to. In this Christ is able to save to the uttermost and willing to save even the chief of sinners, and he welcomes all that penitently come to him for salvation.

Why, then, is this work called "The Blessed God?" In resolving briefly and plainly the conceptions we ought to have of God, we find the revelation of himself to us to *show forth* his eternal blessedness and how that eternal blessedness can become ours in part, *i.e.* that we can experience eternal happiness in the Christ *by knowing him.*

And this is far more than merely knowing about him, as the demons do.[2] Yet, in this, we give praise to God as the blessed One first by having biblical conceptions of his reality (that we understand in part), and then we consider how the blessed God makes us blessed (by bestowing eternal life on those who know him intimately). In eternal life, in abundant life, he *renders* blessings upon all those that hear his voice through his Son.[3] To hold steadfastly to the knowledge of God and of his salvation, is indispensably necessary to our eternal salvation, the glorification of the Christ, and honor we owe to the blessed God. This blessed God, then, will make us happy by these truths, and eternally blessed by them in the power of his Holy Spirit; for these show God's loveliness and blessedness to all that will listen.[4]

In the grace of the Blessed God,
C. Matthew McMahon, Ph.D., Th.D.
From my study, November, 2020

---

[2] "Thou believest that there is one God; thou doest well: the devils also believe, and tremble," (James 2:19). And, "I know thee who thou art, the Holy One of God," (Mark 1:24).

[3] "...and they that hear shall live," (John 5:25).

[4] "My sheep hear my voice, and I know them, and they follow me: And I give unto them eternal life; and they shall never perish, neither shall any man pluck them out of my hand," (John 10:27-28).

Meet Daniel Burgess
Edited by C. Matthew McMahon, Ph.D., Th.D.

Daniel Burgess (1645-1713) was a Calvinistic Presbyterian minister. He was born at Staines, Middlesex, in 1645. His father, also named Daniel Burgess, who, after holding the livings of Staines and of Sutton Magna, Wiltshire, was appointed rector of Collingbourn Ducis, Wiltshire, through the influence of his brother Isaac Burgess, high sheriff of the county. He was ejected in 1662, and was probably the author of the sermon on Eccl. 12:1 (1660, fol.) mentioned by Watts and Allibone. Burgess was placed under Busby at Westminster School in 1654, and entered as a commoner of Magdalen Hall, Oxford, in 1660. He studied hard, but did not graduate, declining to conform. The statement that he took orders at Oxford needs confirmation; he may have had deacon's orders, but more probably only the license of a presbytery.

Leaving the university, he acted as domestic chaplain to Foyl of Chute, Wiltshire, and afterwards to Smith of Tedworth. In 1667 Roger Boyle, first earl of Orrery, lord president of Munster, took him to Ireland, where he remained seven years. He was head master of the school founded by Lord Orrery at Charleville, Cork, and had pupils from the Irish nobility and gentry. He afterwards acted as chaplain to Lady Mervin, near Dublin.

Later, he was ordained by the Dublin presbytery. In Dublin he also married. In 1674 his father's state of health took him to Marlborough; he preached there, and in the neighborhood, and was sent to Marlborough jail. He came to London in his fortieth year (1685), and ministered to a large congregation at a hired meeting-place in Brydges Street, Covent Garden.

Burgess had influential friends; the Countess of Warwick chose him as tutor for her grandson, the future Lord Bolingbroke: in July 1688 Rotheram, one of the new barons of exchequer, took him as his chaplain on the Oxford circuit (in a letter in Rep. of Hist. Manuscripts Commission, p. 378, Burgess is described as "a man of extraordinary ripe parts"), and in 1695 he preached the funeral sermon for the Countess of Ranelagh.

His congregation moved in 1695 to a meeting-house in Russell Court, Drury Lane, and in 1705 a meeting-house was built for him in New Court, Carey Street, Lincoln's Inn Fields. Before it was paid for differences arose in his congregation, ending in a large secession from his ministry. On March 1, 1710 the Sacheverell mob gutted Burgess's meeting-house, and made a bonfire of its pulpit and other fittings. The government offered a reward of 100£. for the apprehension of the rioters, and repaired the building.

Burgess's fame as a preacher was great, and his exuberant animation was something new in the London pulpit. He was a conspicuous example of pith and vivacity at a time when a dry dignity was beginning to be exacted of preachers as a virtue. Mr. Swift, who admits his ability, unjustly taxes him with mixing unction with "incoherence and ribaldry." Tom Brown, says of him in his sermons that he had a "pop-gun way of delivery" which was in harmony with his style of composition. It is full of epigram, terse, quaint, and clear, and never meaningless or dull.

Among current stories of his pulpit wit, the best is that which makes him say that the Jews were called Israelites because God did not choose that. His people should be called Jacobites. His very sensible discourse on "Foolish Talking and Jesting Described and Condemned" (on Eph. 5:4), 1694, 16mo, is in view of his own practice and reputation. Briefly, he contends that "no jesting is lawful but what is medicinal, and restorative of spirits for nobler thoughts."[5] Overall, in theology he was Calvinistic, following Calvin's *Institutes of the Christian Religion*.

Burgess's last years were damped by the defection from his flock and by sickness. "If I must be idle," he said, "I had rather be idle underground than idle above ground." He died on Jan. 26, 1713, and was buried on January 31 in the church of St. Clement Danes. Matthew Henry preached his funeral sermon. Burgess married a Mrs. Briscoe, and had two daughters and a son.

---

[5] That work is an excellent encouragement to Christians in the practice itself, and has been republished by Puritan Publications

Of Burgess' publications there is an imperfect list of thirty-two, beginning with "Soliloquies" which he printed in Ireland, and ending with a Latin defense of nonconformity, called "Appellatio ad Fratres exteros." Among his works are the following:

1. "A Call to Sinners," 1689, 8vo (Written at the request of Baron Rotheram, for the use of condemned criminals).
2. "Seasonable Words for English Protestants," 1690, 4to.
3. "The Character of a Godly Man," 1691, 8vo. *Republished by Puritan Publications.*
4. "Eighteen Directions for Saving Conversion to God," 1691, 8vo.
5. "The Death and Rest, Resurrection and blessed Portion of the Saints" (Dan. 12:13), 1692, 12mo.
6. "A Discourse of the Death and Resurrection of good Men's Bodies," 1692, 8vo.
7. "The Confirming Work of Religion," 1693, 5vo.
8. "The Sure Way to Wealth...even while Taxes rise and Trades sink," 1693, 8vo.
9. "Rules for hearing the Word of God," etc., 2nd ed. 1693, 8vo.
10. "Holy Union and Holy Contention, etc." 1695, 8vo.
11. "Rules and Motives to Holy Prayer," 1696, 8vo.
12. "Causa Dei; or Counsel to the Rich," 1697, 8vo.
13. "The Golden Snuffers," Exod. 37:23, 1697, 12mo (a favorite illustration with him, see Foolish Talking. This was the first sermon preached to the Societies for the Reformation of

Manners). He superintended the third edition (?1681) of Robert Fleming"s "The Fulfilling of the Scripture,"

14. The famous whig tract, "The Craftsmen: a Sermon, composed by the late Daniel Burgess, and intended to be preached by him in the High Times, but prevented by the Burning of his Meeting House," in "Indep. Whig," ii. 236, and separate, 2nd ed. 1720, 8vo, is by Thomas Gordon.

15. "Foolish Jesting Described," Republished by Puritan Publications.

16. "The Blessed God," 1688; this current volume.[6]

17. "Directions for Daily Holy Living," Republished by Puritan Publications.

For Further Study:

Henry's *Funeral Sermon for Burgess*, 1713; Calamy's *Continuation*, 1727, p. 872; Walker's *Sufferings of the Clergy*, 1714. ii. 92 (wrongly numbered 94), 336, 373; Palmer's *Nonconf. Memorial*, 1802, pp. 296, 330; *Prot. Diss.*

---

[6] *The Blessed God* by Daniel Burgess (1645-1713), Three questions resolved briefly and plainly, *viz.* What conceptions ought we to have of the blessed God? What are those truths, whereof the knowledge appeareth most indispensably necessary unto our salvation; and (therefore) to be first and most learnt by us? What is the change wrought in a man by God's holy Word and Spirit, before he can safely conclude himself passed from death to life? Being the sum of three sermons. John 21:15, "Jesus saith unto him, feed my lambs," (*i.e.* souls, even the lowest.) 1 Cor. 3.2, "I have fed you with milk, and not with meat," (*i.e.* Doctrine fit for weaklings, not folk of strong understanding.) (London: printed for Thomas Parkhurst at the bible and three crowns, at the lower end of Cheapside, and Robert Gibbs at the golden ball in chancery-lane. 1688).

Mag. vol. vi.; Bogus and Bennett's *Hist. of Dissenters*, 1809, ii, 270 seq.; Salmon's *Chron. Hist.* 1733, p. 320; T. Browtfs *Works*, 9th ed. 1760, iii. 100; Caufield's *Portraits*, 1819, i. 52; Calamy's *Hist. Account of my own Life*, 2nd ed. 1830, ii. 465 seq.; Walter Wilson's MSS. in Dr. William's Library.

To the Congregation Under My Care

It is said, my brethren, that whatever affections are in the middle will have two sharp ends.

Our first love has been as zealous as our first knowledge was wondrous. I am persuaded also that when we are parted, it will be no less ardent; that our separation will be as painful as it would be if our limbs were separated from our body. May we take care that while we are kept together by good providence, we allow no lessening in that sweet and useful grace of godly love by showing it to be like the unchangeable love of God.

The greatest thing I can give you is my love. Next to that is my labor. But my talent which is lean is shorter than my desire. Without your very great affection, I can expect little success of my preaching or writing. By this I am encouraged toward both, and in both, as it is that which has given *the imprimatur* to these notes. The truths of God that are in them I study and think about most honorably. And as to anything that is mine in them, I praise God that I am prepared to hear other's criticisms.

Neither do I purpose to put you off with these fragments. But I promise you that if the Lord will, and I live, I will fulfill the debt I owe you for the whole. I must beg your patience, however, for some time, though I need not say for what reasons, since all that know me know them also.

My days on earth may be few. Be whether they are more or less, the greatest part of them shall be spent in labors and prayers for you and your families. As long as I am capable of either, you, more than any others, shall have them. For this reason, I ask for your prayers for me, and I know you have other motives. So, I know I can expect them.

I am an affectionate servant of your faith, obedience and joy,
DANIEL BURGESS

Part 1:
Truths About God

Question 1: What conceptions should we have of the blessed God?

Of all truths, the most evident is that there *is* a God. And of all things knowable, it is most necessary that we know who he is. To know him perfectly is impossible, of course. An oyster shell cannot contain the ocean, nor can a finite mind comprehend an infinite object. Only God himself can fully know himself. But he made our minds to know him, with a knowledge sufficient to serve and enjoy him. We are capable of this much. For this he promised us plentiful means and aids. And without this, every mother's child must be everlastingly miserable.

Our thoughts of him are the seed of all our affections, words, and conversation toward him and toward one another. If these are corrupt, nothing is sound of all that is in us or comes from us. Nor can these be good, unless they are true and agreeable, powerful, and answerable to their end. God's own Word is the measure for them, in addition to the revelation of him in nature, and Scripture published.

The end of them is the exaltation of God's name, the subjection of us to his authority, and the inclination of us to obey his law. When our thoughts follow this rule and obtain this end, our conceptions of God are what they should be.

Indeed, revelation is the measure of faith God requires in exchange for what he gives. He gives some a hundredfold more advantages for knowing him than he bestows on others. And he will accept a hundredfold less from some men than others. Let ministers, rich men, and such as sit under the best ministry of the Word remember this and tremble. Let the unlearned, the poor, and those that live meagerly under the worst ministry think of this, and in hope get all they are able to get.

Nevertheless, let us all consider that we all have the great volume of the world that the heathens had. We have what Moses, the prophets, and the Jews had. In addition, we have Christ and his apostles, and the gospel light, that they did not have. Yes, and we have many displays of it in our country, as the very churches beyond the seas do not have. (I wish our city's advantages were better observed by us.) Much is given to our country, very much to our city. And the thoughts of himself that God will require from us Englishmen, and especially Londoners, must be presumed to extend to these sixteen particulars.

Seven concerning his essence, three concerning the relationship he has with all his creatures, and six concerning the special relationship he has with us believers. If anyone seems excusable, I ask the reader to give me his reason. If this seems impossible to understand and hold in memory, I desire that it be thought of as true as I can make it appear. I could find ten-year-old children who can easily and sufficiently understand and retain these points in their memories. And if grown people cannot do so, they must blame their own reprobate mind. Read on, you who have will and power.

Concerning God's essence or nature, in order to know who, what, and how he is different from all other beings, we must remember these truths.

1. He is an uncaused, or unmade being. A creature is a thing contrived by God's wisdom, made from nothing by his power, and this freely, of his own will and choice. But God is a being that never came out of not-being. He was never contrived by his own or any other wisdom. He was never made by his own or any other power and will. In truth, all the world would agree that a thing cannot be the cause of itself, as that is impossible. And for a creature or second being to be the cause of its God or first being, is such an absurdity that no mind would even consider it. That which is nothing can do nothing. If there was a time when God was nothing, surely at that time he could do nothing. And if so, he could not make himself. As for other causes, I ask as the apostle does in another case, "who hath first given to him, and it shall be recompensed?" (Rom. 11:35).

2. He is an eternal being. A creature is a thing that has a morn, a noon, and a night, or you might say a beginning, a change, and an end. That end includes a return to its initial nothingness the first moment that God ceases to uphold it. Angels and our souls are of themselves mortal, and it is only by divine will, power, and sustenance that they are immortal (Heb. 1:3). But God is Jehovah. His being shall be, is, and has ever been. He is without beginning (Ps. 90:2), without change (Ps. 102:27), and without end (Ps. 102:26).

3. He is an independent being. A creature is a thing that cannot stand alone. Material, mixed, and spiritual

creatures all are weak, all are unable to sustain themselves or produce themselves. But God is a being that's above dependency. He did not come into being by any help, and he does not continue being by any help or outside support. He depends on nothing (Gen. 17:1). He is *El Shaddai,* God all-sufficient. He is all, so that he can need nothing; he is all, so that he can support everything.

4. He is a necessary being. A creature is a thing that may or may not be. What must be, or must not be, is as God pleases (Rev. 4:11). But God is a being that cannot *but be.* One to which it is eternally repugnant and impossible either never to have been or to cease from being. One who only has being and immortality necessarily (1 Tim. 6:16). One whose being and immortality never required one act of his will or power, nor are capable of being made to cease.

5. He is an all-perfect being. A creature is a thing of imperfection in every reference. This imperfect being has more lack than substance. Every creature is imperfect in all. And no one creature has all the perfections that divine goodness has dispersed among all. But God is a being of excellent perfection, and perfection in every excellency. Everyone conceived by men and angels, and whatever is inconceivable, God is above the blessing and praise of both (Neh. 9:5). He is above all that he has revealed himself to us to be, and more than is revealed, or possible to be revealed, to us finite creatures.[7] God cannot be better or greater than

---

[7] See the *1647 Westminster Larger Catechism* and Mr. Charnock on the *Divine Attributes.*

he is, and finite minds must conclude that he is infinitely above all that they can hope to ever conceive.

6. He is a triune being. That is, he is a being that subsists in three distinct persons. Here is the mystery of mysteries. It may be the hardest to understand, but easy as any to be believed. With such brightness it is revealed in the blessed gospel. How necessary it is to be believed is evident in this: (1.) This manner of being is the topmost glory of God. It is the best manner of being that can be, without which it is hard to think how God should be in himself infinitely glorious or blessed. His creatures are, and can only be finite, and yet the infinite glory of the divine persons shines in their relations one to the other. Their blessedness consists in their loving and being loved of one another.[8] (2.) The doctrine of God's subsisting in, or being Father, Son, and Spirit distinctly is most firmly rooted in all aspects of our Christian religion. For this reason, if ignorance or unbelief of the glorious trinity exists in us, our Christianity is lost. And it would necessarily be another gospel, even a high road to sin and hell, that we would be pursuing.[9] A tree is one, and yet its root, trunk, and branch are three. Each of these has its own manner of being. The root is of itself, the trunk is of the root, the branches are from both root and trunk. They give forth fruit in a threefold manner: the root originally and firstly, the trunk continually, and then the branch completely and immediately. Who cannot apply

---

[8] Dr. Francis Cheynell on *the Trinity* in chapter 5 deserves a good reading.
[9] See Matt. 28:19, 1 John 5:7, John 14:26, John 15:26.

this? God is one. This one God is Father, Son, and Spirit: three persons. The Father is of himself. The Son is of the Father. The Holy Spirit is of the Father and Son. In the communication of good, they all work jointly, yet there are distinct personal operations by which they make way for the glory of each other. Inception or beginning of good is from the Father, dispensation is by the Son, and consummation or completing is by the Spirit. I do not forget and would have my reader remember this often quoted saying, namely, "All comparisons, though helpful, are yet disproportionate." It is very true; no similitude can match the thing; but this, and others like it, may help our understandings.

7. He is the all-working being that foreordains whatever comes to pass and effects whatever he foreordains. Regarding works of creation and providence, a creature is a thing that cannot itself come from nothing into being. Neither can it afterward uphold its being, virtues, or actions. It cannot govern itself (Acts 17:28). It cannot be independent regarding its sustenance or being. But God is a being, all-working. His Word speaks all into being; his conserving influence goes to our preservation; his assisting influence maintains our operation. His assisting influence or concurrence foregoes the operation of creatures, in order though not in time. It is his cooperation, or co-working with the creature, that produces many effects and fulfills his sovereign will. Without the creature's operation, God will not produce many effects, and without God's cooperation, the creature cannot produce anything at all. God's co-

working is also immediate. Without the assistance of his immediate virtue and power and presence, there could be no effect. He is called *hamakom*, or "the place" as he is present everywhere always. Lastly, he is determining. There can be but one absolute determiner and over-ruler of operations. And who is this but God? And, if by him the operations of creatures were not absolutely determined, it would be very possible that he might be frustrated and disappointed at his ends sometimes. But there is nothing more impossible than that. Observe that in this sense, God works all things; and he does this without changing the nature of things or offering violence to them. He allows them to act by and under him, as freely as though there were no decree upon them or hand overruling them.[10]

Concerning God's relationships that are common to all his creatures, let us note what follows.

1. He is the supreme benefactor. Creatures can only be the bearers of his benefits to us. The benefactor is God. All the good we have ever had, have, and shall ever have, God contrives, wills, and executes. He begins all, carries on all, and completes all freely without necessity and graciously without merit.

2. He is the supreme ruler. Creatures have no power or authority but from him, and under him, and for him, making him most fit to rule. His creation and conservation of all things give him infinite right and title to rule all, to

---

[10] See Mr. Norton's *Orthodox Evangelist.*

make laws, to judge according to those laws, and to execute judgment so passed.

3. He is the absolute proprietor and owner. Creatures are not their own, nor are they one another's. God is entirely his own. And he owns all the works of his hands. Without the shadow of a spot on his justice, he may do what he will with his own, whether person, family, kingdom, church, or world. His authority can no more be disproved than his power can be resisted if he exalts, or debases, or destroys.

Concerning God's special, particular relationships to us believers, I appeal to my readers just how needful it is that the following six things are ever in our deepest and severest thoughts and that concerning God, every one of us is able to say, and keep saying, that...

1. He is my ever-present friend and Father. Even before sin's entrance, he dearly loved me, and that without a mediator, sacrificing and interceding for me. He made me in his likeness naturally, an intelligent and immortal being. He made me in his likeness morally, for holiness, blessedness, and dominion over inferior creatures. He entered into a covenant with me in my first parent, a covenant to sweeten his government and to secure my obedience; a covenant of exceptional terms. This covenant he founded not only in his will but in the very nature of things themselves. For it bound me to be blessed, that is, to be holy. It threatened no evil at all, unless I first committed the worst of all acts which is sin. This was a covenant signed and sealed with sacraments as the trees of knowledge and of life.

2. He is next my angry and armed enemy, and in all appearance irreconcilable. For as soon as I sinned in Adam, he loathed me, and my soul also abhorred him. He then took away his Holy Spirit from me and gave me up to the bondage of the law that I had broken, to the servitude of the sin that I had committed, to the tyranny of Satan to whom I had hearkened, and to the power of death that I now deserved. O the wrath! O the vengeance! And alas! What hope appeared to men, or to angels, of any reconciliation? Neither could imagine a reconcilement to be possible, much less think it future or coming.

3. He is my propitiated God, welcoming and inviting me to reconciliation. Come seize me, O wonder and joy! It is he that gave his co-essential eternal Son for a sin offering for fallen men, though not for fallen angels. An offering that satisfies his justice for all iniquity and merits every mercy. And that so fully, that as a result of this reunion with my maker, I am encouraged, and even commanded, to seek, pray, and wait for all good things without money and without price, and without any quality or work of my own. By his Christ, his Spirit, and his ministers he stoops to intreat and beseech me to be friends with him (2 Cor. 5:20). He has made it now the worst of sins that I am capable of sinning, which is to presume that I am a reprobate. Further, there is no hope for my recovery out of my sin and misery but by his grace in Christ to all offered, without exception.

4. He is, as sure as I repent and believe, my reconciled God. It is he that lays aside all his anger to love me freely, pardon me fully, and accept graciously my soul, saying, "all

that I have is thine," (Luke 15), "and I will be thy God." And all this in the first instant that I mourn for, and turn from my sin, to believe on his Son, resigning myself to be taught, saved, and ruled by him. He then turns from all his judicial wrath. And when I live up unto the grace received by me, he turns from all his paternal or fatherly displeasure. He only withdraws his assistance of me when I willfully and presumptuously sin against him. He further spares me from sins of unbeatable infirmity and attack, as a father does for the son that desires to serve him.

  5. He is both my reconciled and my covenanted God. He never dealt with man in any other way than this most sweet one of covenant! Hallowed be his name! And it is he that now has well bound himself to be my God, as me to be his servant. It is he that to my wondrous advantages has covenanted with me. (1.) He has covenanted with me doubly. First in my parents, promising me mercy for their sakes (Rom. 11:28), and promising them mercy for me as well (Exod. 20:6). And secondly, in my person. He has made a covenant with me (2 Sam. 23:5, Ezek. 16:8). (2.) He covenanted with me sacramentally. Sacraments are signs and seals on God's part, bonds and badges on our parts (Rom. 4:11, 1 Cor. 20:16). Bless his name, O my soul! He has visibly covenanted with me in holy baptism and at his holy table. (3.) He has covenanted with me with signs and seals early, based on my original sin, even in my very infancy before I could commit an actual sin. Also, before I could desire grace, he demonstrated the freeness of his grace. I was baptized early and encouraged and engaged to obey the

gospel when I came to years of capacity, so that I cannot but see God's kindness in forestalling Satan's seductions. And all the days of my life I will remember it, as David does in Psalm 22:10, "Thou art my God, (*that is, my covenant God*) from my mother's belly. Thou didst make me to hope when I was on my mother's breasts." In other words, by the covenant then signed and sealed for me, God laid the foundations and motives for my hope in him when I should come of understanding. (4.) He has signed and sealed covenant with me frequently. I am no stranger at his table. I have eaten of his holy bread often and received nourishment from it.

6. He is my God, engaged to me by pawns and pledges. Signs and seals are wonderful appendices to divine promises. God has given me the highest, most solemn, and sweetest testimonies of his will to forever be my God and portion. The earnest of his Spirit, with his blessed graces and consolations, ensure all the good things of the covenant. These are the first fruits that make the best security for the whole harvest. And these, grace has made my own.

And now I beg pardon in my Savior's blood for all the defects of this paper. They whose letters and messages have extracted it I ask to pardon and accept it. Let them, with me, ever remember this saying of the great light of our age, that the sun may more easily be included in a spark of fire, than the infinite perfections of God be comprehended in a finite mind.

Part 2:
Truths Necessary for Salvation

Question 2: What are those truths of the knowledge of God which appear indispensably necessary and spiritually desirable to our salvation?

All true Christians know some biblical truths, for there are truths we must necessarily know if we are to become a Christian (Isa. 27:11). Those truths that are given for our comfort and usefulness to ourselves and others are given for our salvation, though not necessarily for working out the same.

It does not seem that God desires us to know what all these truths are nor how many of them there are, because understanding every truth would be inconsistent with both reason and grace.

It is enough for us to know the essential and integral doctrines which enriched the Christians gone to heaven before us, and God has revealed in his Word what these are. And from his holy Word I will now attempt to declare what they are in a comprehensive, clear, and yet concise manner.

Foundationally, sanctification is salvation begun; salvation is sanctification perfected. Grace and glory differ only in degree. What is necessary for the one is also essential for the other. Sanctification is our conformity to God through Jesus Christ, and is accomplished by the covenant of grace. Those truths which most directly lead to this end are of the greatest weight and importance, and so should be attended to in the first place. For this reason, I have commended these seven articles to be first learned, even before any catechism itself.

Answer 1. God the Father, Son, and Spirit created the world. He created man, wise, holy, blessed, and honorable. He covenanted with the first man, and with his future generations after him, that if they obeyed perfectly, they should be forever happy. And if they sinned, they should die. This is called the covenant of works.

Answer 2. Adam the first man, and his posterity in him, breached that covenant, and by this fell under God's wrath, the curse of sin, and Satan's power.

Answer 3. From eternity, God the Father covenanted with his Son, Jesus Christ, for the redemption of sinners from sin and misery. By taking on the form of a man and a servant, Christ became a curse and afterward an intercessor for them. This is called the Covenant of Redemption, or redemption covenant.

Answer 4. In pursuance of this redemption covenant, Christ the Savior was preached. And in him, wisdom, righteousness, sanctification, and redemption offered through repentance, faith in God through him, and new obedience. This is called the Covenant of Grace.

Answer 5. For us to believe God's promises to us in the Covenant of Grace, and for our further engagement to fulfil the demands from us in it, God was pleased to solemnize this covenant by some outward rites and ceremonies of his own appointment. And the ceremonies he appointed for these ends in the New Testament church are baptism and the Lord's Supper. These are called therefore, the signs and seals of the covenant.

Answer 6. Obedience to the gospel through faith in Christ and by the help of the Holy Spirit is necessary for all that have inwardly consented to the covenant of grace and outwardly solemnized between God and them with baptism and the Lord's Supper.

Answer 7. Those who are inside the Covenant of Grace will be rewarded into eternity, while those who are outside will be punished into eternity, in both soul and body.

An attentive mind will comprehend the following articles. Further, I judge that a skillful teacher would be the most apt for explaining and applying these truths.

Point 1. The object of saving truth is best considered by inquirers after truth.

Point 2. The authority and sufficiency of the Old and New Testaments of our Lord Jesus Christ, as penned by Moses and the prophets, the evangelists and apostles are certain.

Point 3. The object is he whose name is glorious, above all blessing and praise, for his singular essence, subsisting in three distinct persons.

Point 4. The outward works of God are creation and providence. One is God's giving first being to all things. The other is his preserving and ordering them unto his own wise and holy end.

Point 5. God's general providence is over all things. His principal is over men and angels.

Point 6. God's providence over man respects man's fourfold estate of knowledge: innocence, misery, grace, and glory.

Point 7. Regarding grace toward man, election and redemption are of utmost consideration. The vessels are God's church and people. The degrees are vocation, justification, sanctification. The means are the Word, sacraments, and prayer.

Point 8. Regarding the glory God confers on his children, observe these four steps. Assurance of eternal love that was first obtained; heavenly mansions that will be possessed from the day of death to the day of judgment; honor that will be granted at the day of judgment; complete glory that will be bestowed after the day of general judgment and will endure forever.

Trial will best indicate how, with small pains and great profit, this anthology may be obtained. And when through understanding and memory it is obtained, I advise that the following twelve points should be studied, namely, three concerning God, three concerning man, three concerning Christ, and three concerning the application of Christ for salvation.

Point 1. There is one only God, an infinite, perfect, and spiritual essence.

Point 2. This one God is Father, Son and Spirit, distinguished into three manners of subsistence, after a way incomprehensible. The Father eternally begetting, the Son begotten, the Holy Spirit proceeding.

Point 3. This one God is the maker, preserver, and governor of all things by infinite wisdom, power, and goodness.

Point 4. Man was made of such a body and soul that he was able to have attained eternal life for himself and his posterity had he continued obedient.

Point 5. Man, in this way made, was envied and tempted by the devil, and yielded willfully to his temptation. In doing so, he broke the law and covenant of God and made himself and all his posterity cursed by God, slaves to sin and Satan, unable to escape the threatened death.

Point 6. Man, in this way completely impoverished and pitied by God who, in prosecution of an eternal counsel and covenant of peace, provided a Savior to him, even Jesus Christ the righteous.

Point 7. Jesus Christ, this Savior, is, as to his natures, perfect God, and perfect man in one person; and as to his offices, he is prophet, priest and king in both his states of humiliation and exaltation.

Point 8. Jesus Christ's humiliation in being made under the law, obeying the precepts, and suffering the curse of it, was deeper than any mere creature could possibly undergo. And his exaltation, in rising from the dead as he did, ascending into heaven, and having all power in heaven and earth given him, was higher than any mere creature could possibly be exalted to.

Point 9. Jesus Christ, being so exalted, is able to save to the uttermost and willing to save even the chief of sinners.

Part 2: Truths Necessary for Salvation

He welcomes all that penitently come to him and mourns over all that obstinately keep away from him.

Point 10. Application of Christ to produce our salvation by him is twofold. Namely, application is made both by God and by ourselves. God applies Christ to us by his Holy Spirit, when by him he gives us will and power to embrace him as offered in the gospel. We apply Christ to ourselves when by faith worked in us, we embrace him as prophet, priest, and king, covenanting with him to be such forever.

Point 11. Application of Christ as described should be sought, prayed and waited for by every soul using all God's appointed means without rest until they have through grace attained it.

Point 12. Application of Christ outside of the means appointed by God cannot be hoped for, but in the constant and diligent use of those means, no man need fear that he shall not find it.

When novices have gotten this far, they are more than a little advantaged to learn any of our catechisms. Yet let me say that I would not have that, or any other, singularly addressed.

All methods of categorizing truths are imperfect; but I say that the Creed, the Lord's Prayer, the Ten Commandments, and the doctrine of the sacraments make the most complete body of truths that we can form. The guide for our faith is found in the Creed, the guide for our prayers in the Lord's Prayer, the guide for our practice in the Ten Commandments, and the great encouragement and engagement to believe, pray, and live holy is found in the doctrine of the sacraments. I conclude, therefore, using such a small map of the world of truths as these that we can be greatly benefited. What follows is the list of the 12 Tenants in the Creed.

    1. There is a God, and he is three distinct persons whose revelations of himself are to be credited, his promises relied on, and his demands from us heartily and practically consented to. And the first person of these three (first in order, though not in time, of being, and working) is the Father. He is the Father of all things by creation, of his church by adoption, of his Christ by generation in time, as he was man; and by generation eternal and inconceivable, as he is God. He is the Father almighty, regarding his right to do whatever he pleases, and possessing all power and strength to do it with. He is maker of heaven and earth, that is, of all things and of the university of beings.

    2. The second person of the godhead is, as to office, Jesus. He is the Savior from sin by price, by prayer and by power. As to his authority, he is Christ, set apart by God, qualified, and commissioned to be a saving Prophet, Priest, and King. As to his essence and relation to God the Father, he is his only Son by eternal, natural, inconceivable generation. As to his supremacy and honor, he is our Lord by natural right, as he is God, and by delegated right, as he is the Lord to whom all dominion is given. This presents a double consideration because of the price he paid to purchase it from God, and because of the victory by which he gained it all from creatures.

3. This Christ, as man, was without human father. Conceived, or prepared, by the Holy Spirit who first miraculously sanctified a portion of the virgin mother's flesh and blood, and then fashioned his sinless body. Christ was born of that virgin Mary, according to the prophecy in Isaiah 7:14.[11] Mary was a princess by extraction, a descendant of king David and father Abraham. Yet she was poor, espoused to a carpenter, a holy and humble creature. Notably, Mary was never called "mother" by our Savior himself.

4. This Christ suffered at the hands of God, men, and devils, in soul and body, name and friends. Under Pontius Pilate, in the time of his presidency under Tiberius Caesar, this same Christ was crucified, a manner of death used by the Romans in that day that was especially cursed by God. He died, was buried, and descended into hell; that is, his soul and body were separated from each other, though neither was separated from the godhead at all. His body was buried the same day he died. And for part of three days, about thirty-eight or forty hours in all, his body was apart from his soul.

5. The third day (after his death) he rose again from the dead by his Father's power (Rom. 6:4), by his own power (John 2:19), by the Holy Spirit's power (1 Peter 3:18), and by the collective power of all the divine persons. Otherwise, he could not have saved one soul (1 Cor. 15:13-14).

---

[11] "Therefore the Lord himself shall give you a sign; Behold, a virgin shall conceive, and bear a son, and shall call his name Immanuel," (Isa. 7:14).

6. This Christ, forty days after his resurrection, ascended into heaven (Enoch and Elijah did the same as Old Testament types of Christ) in plain view of his disciples. He now sits at the right hand of God the Father almighty; that is, he is next to God in dignity, power, and glory. And under God, he administers all things. Sitting indicates security, rest, and honorable dominion.

7. This same Christ shall come to judge those that are alive at the last day as well as all that have died before that time. It is true that God, as God, is Judge supreme at judgment day. Christ as Mediator is the delegated, constitutional judge who pronounces sentence. And his very saints are judges by accession and approval of his sentence. It must not be forgotten that he judges every one of us when we die though not all of us together, nor with execution of all his judgment upon our souls and bodies, until the last day.

8. The third person of the godhead is the Holy Ghost, signifying breath, or spirit. This glorious person bears this name with a specialty, as he is eternally and inconceivably breathed forth from the Father and Son. And like the other two members of the godhead, he is holy; he is the worker of all renewed holiness in fallen man.

9. This Father, Son and Spirit have a holy church. This church is made up of all those who are called forth of both the Gentile and Jewish worlds by God's Word and Spirit. After mention of the Holy Spirit, the church is referred to in our creed as *a work* of the Holy Spirit. It is a universal body, because the New Testament church consists

of people of all nations, in contrast to the Jewish church which was confined to one nation. It encompasses all Christians of all ages, past, present, and future in the world, which are indeed but one body (Eph. 4:3-6). It is said to be holy as, 1. Christ who is holy is its head. 2. The blessed Spirit who is holy is its indweller. 3. The gospel, which is holy, is its rule. 4. All true members of this church are imperfectly holy. 5. Their minister's office is holy. 6. Their worship, as God's ordinance, is holy. 7. All baptized members are sacramentally, though not spiritually, holy as they are bound to the gospel, though they do not fully obey it.

10. The communion of saints is the effect of the Holy Spirit's sanctifying of them. Saints are those who are separated from an unclean life and carried by the virtue of infused grace to the fear, love, and service of God in Christ. Communion between the members of the body is established on the following tenants: 1. A common holy friendship with Father, Son and Spirit. 2. Their mutual love of one another as themselves. 3. Their care and just labor for each other's welfare. 4. Their joining with one heart and soul in God's public worship by Christ ordained.

And the saints of this communion have forgiveness of their sins. On the satisfaction and merit of Christ's obedience and intercession, God pronounces them acquitted and delivers them from the execution of their sin's just punishment. God may be said to punish, or discipline, his children, but not in payment for their sins; it is for their good that God ever chastens them.

11. These saints must also hereafter experience the resurrection of their bodies and, by consequence, they have immortal souls. For otherwise, of what use would the bodies be? All objections against this said resurrection are therefore in vain seeing that it is so brightly revealed in scripture.

12. Life everlasting is the saint's portion, perfect duration without change or end. In contrast, we may determine that sinners dying in their sins shall have the contrary, which is everlasting death, or eternal evil.

Does it seem strange that the reward of short and slender obedience should be so immense and everlasting? And the punishment of finite creature's sin, in a few years committed, should be of such extremity and through all eternity? The wonder vanishes when you consider the greatness of the God who orders the punishment and the reward. A great God does all things great and like himself. His rewards must be great, and his punishments great. They would otherwise be a reproach to him.

I most certainly and verily believe these things on divine revelation, though they exceed the reach of my sense and my reason.

In the Lord's Prayer there are eight truths to know.

1. There is a God eternal, from whom we may and ought to request the supply of all our needs, as a child does his father. For though he is in heaven and by this of incomprehensible perfection and cannot without a great condescension even regard or affect the best of creatures, yet he is the Father of all creation and the Father of Christ through whom we are redeemed. He is the Father of

penitent believers by both regeneration and adoption. Bare needs do not destroy men. It is the neglect of a right relationship to the Lord (that he is Father, that he is the heavenly Father, and that he is *our* heavenly Father) that can and does undo the world.

2. Exaltation of God's name, subjection to his authority, and obedience to his will and precepts, are the chief end of man. He made us for these. And for these he redeemed us. For these by his Word and Spirit he calls us. For these we live. Yet all men are insufficient for them all. For the will, skill, and power to do these, all men are to pray unto him.

3. "Bread," or the necessaries of this life, pardon for sin, and preventive grace restraining from sin are the means to that end – this exaltation, subjection, and obedience. It is self-idolatry to desire one bit of bread, or the pardon of one sin, or the victory over one temptation, either singularly or principally for our own ends, in order that our bodies or our souls, our reputation or our estates may not suffer. But for these ends they must be not only desired but prayed for, begged for with all humble importunity. We are infinitely unworthy of them. Our prayers do not deserve God's bestowing them. But prayer is the only way in which God warrants our expectation of them and in which he gives ground to expect them without doubting. His omnipotence is honored by free grace accompanied with holy prayer.

4. Conservation of our beings is the first of our personal wants; pardon for sin is the second; deliverance from temptation and sin is the third. Make a note of this

order. And desire them in this order. For if God does not preserve our being, we are then incapable of doing and receiving any good. Therefore, it is our being that we must first pray for. If God does not pardon our sins, our being is cursed and worse than none at all. For we cannot avoid his wrath, which is the hell of hell. Therefore, pardon is what we should pray for secondly. If God does not deliver us from sinful temptation's prevalence, our being and past pardon are very sorry things. For sin, after pardon, is worse sin; and this will kindle a worse wrath of God. And what then becomes of us? Therefore, deliverance from sin and the temptation to sin is what we must pray for next. We pray for all these; and in this natural method that our dear redeemer teaches.

5. High and honorable thoughts of God must be in the minds of all that pray to him and must be expressed at the beginning of their prayer. The preface to the Lord's prayer teaches us this. "Father" signifies creator, ruler, benefactor. These words, "art in heaven," do not speak to where God dwells, for he is everywhere, filling every place and space. Instead, these words signify God's eternal perfection, as far above our minds as the heavens are above the earth. "Our Father" also speaks much in that it demonstrates him to be the Father of both creation and the church.

6. "Kingdom, power, and glory" are the three steps by which our minds rise in the praise of God. Kingdom signifies his just right to govern all things. Power signifies his perfect strength with which he does it. Glory signifies

the shining excellency of his perfections. We should conceive of God as a ruler most rightful, powerful, amiable, and beautiful.

7. Praise, the highest of all worship, must not be sparingly used in prayer. The preface and conclusion of the Lord's Prayer are as full of praise as the heavens are of stars! And no wonder, for greatness and goodness encompass all God's perfections. Thanksgiving is a noble form of worship that honors divine goodness. Praise exalts God as great and can never be practiced enough by us.[12]

8. Prayer is to be ended with "amen" in the same way it is to be begun with "our Father." In other words, it must be concluded with desire, faith and hope. "Amen" signifies everything. Apathy, unbelief, and a lack of waiting before God destroys prayer. Without the heart's actual "amen" after prayer, you are basically saying, "Lord, my mind is already set. I am indifferent to your answer, whether you grant or deny me. I believe you will deny me. And I will not wait or look for your answer."

It is certain, where holy *amens* are not found, prayers will be lost.

Commandment truths include these twelve tenants.

1. The object to whom all supreme worship is to be paid is God alone. To him it must be paid by all souls, in all times, with all strength, and to no other. It is treason to pay a penny tribute to a rebellious usurper or to give divine worship to any creature. If Jesus Christ is not God by eternal

---

[12] See Psalm 50.

nature, I would not be baptized in his name or pray to him, any more than I would pray to a star.

2. It is as necessary that God is the Author, as well as the Object of all religious worship. We must give him no worship other than that prescribed by his Word. His worship must suit his blessed nature and will. And who can know these apart from his Word?

3. It is not enough to worship the true God for its matter; the manner in which we worship also must be far from profane. It must be with holy reverence and humble spirit and hearty truth.

4. It is not enough to worship the true God by the true rule, in the true and right manner; we must also keep holy a certain portion of every day and every week. Holy observance of the Lord's Day, and of hours of worship on our own days, is the practice and pleasure of sincere men.

5. Obedience to all the former commands are not enough on their own without duty to men, and especially to superiors. Principally, we are to honor our natural parents for they are our original governors on a deeper foundation than that of any contract, as we are their very nature. To them are we most obliged, and by them we are most loved. If only children and parents would do their duties toward each other, our families, and consequently our churches, could be rescued. Parents and rulers are God's governors over us; and next to God, should be honored by us.

6. Regarding our duty toward man, preservation of just honor is the first; preservation of life is the next. The closer you come to unjustly killing a man, the closer you are

to doing the devil's service, for from the beginning he was a murderer. If you murder a man, you deprive him of all the good of this world, and unless he is already converted, you throw him into hell. If you murder a man, you rob God, the king, and the country, of a servant in this world.

7. The third kind of duty is towards mankind and is a preservation of chastity in ourselves and others. To defile is next to killing; obscene thoughts, words, and deeds are next to murderous ones. Both are odious in God's eyes.

8. The fourth part of our duty towards man is preservation of his estate. To condemn, to kill, or to defile is worse; but to rob and injure in ever so little a matter is a sin that God will not let go unpunished. Of what infamy among men is the name of a thief? O that thieves knew what God thinks of them!

9. The fifth sort of duty to man is preservation of them in their causes and suits of law, by bearing true witness when called and abhorring all false testimony – all that tends to pervert public justice.

10. The sixth duty toward man is to show the same love for him that we show ourselves and to not begrudge him any good, in the same way as we do not begrudge ourselves good. The first command is a summary of all duty unto God; the second is a like summary of all duty unto man.

11. The children of men, ever since the fall, are at enmity with the will of God. Their minds are unteachable, their memories unfaithful, their wills intractable. Else, why did we need the Ten Commandments? (Exod. 19-20).

12. The motives that God gives are the same which we ought to take to heart, even the obedience of every one of God's laws, especially these three that are contained in the preface to the ten commandments: God's sovereignty over us, his covenant with us, and his redemption-grace and bounty unto us.

Now, the sacramental truths are these five:

1. The law of God for sacraments is not natural, but positive. He does not require them because they are good, but they are good because he requires them. Therefore, we must use the sacraments because God commanded them. But at the same time it is possible to use sacraments and not please God because God has commanded them not for their own sakes, but for certain ends which, if we do not aim at in our use of the sacraments, God has no pleasure in our doing of them, and we do not profit by our use of them.

2. The end for which God has ordained sacraments is to testify his mind and will to us, and to testify back our heart toward him. It is true that God's Word is a testimony of his will – a sweet and a sure testimony. But it has pleased him to add a second sort of testimony to his covenant will, and to testify to it further by visible rites and ceremonies of his own appointing. Likewise, at the point of conversion, by our hearts and mouths we testify to God that our will from that point forward is to be his. But it pleases God to require a second and more public, solemn testimony using those rites and ceremonies which he has prescribed. And if we do not aim at both of these ends in the use of sacraments, we

mock God and delude ourselves in their use. There are other ends of sacraments of course, but these are the chief of all.

3. The order of the two sacraments of the gospel is first holy baptism, which demonstrates that a new disciple of Christ by sign and seal is covenanted with God. And secondly, The Lord's Supper, which renews that covenant between God and a baptized disciple of Jesus Christ. Both baptism and the Lord's Supper confirm the covenant, mutually on the part of God and us, and extensively, regarding all the promises in the covenant from God to us, and all the demands in the covenant from us to God.

4. The dignity and usefulness of the holy sacraments are surpassing. In no ordinance has God condescended so low as he has in these. And in none has he so honored us as in these. The apostle reckons sacraments as the prime privilege of the church (1 Cor. 10). As for usefulness, they are towers of David, built for spiritual armories. We cannot expect the Holy Spirit to make the Word helpful to us without the sacraments. If he should so do, he would disparage them. But to be sure, he will never do that.

5. The way to improve the holy sacraments to our own holiness and comfort is by pleading them with our own souls on God's behalf, urging our hearts in such words like, "My soul, my soul, why do you set yourself against God? Or why do you respond so coldly to him?" The kingdom of hell promotes violence, and violent sinners take it by force. Will you not defend the kingdom of heaven with such strength? Sinners forsake father and mother, take up their cross, and follow Satan, and through many tribulations enter the

kingdom of hell. Will you not without regret enter the kingdom of heaven that is better, through tribulations that are lesser? Think, think my soul! You are baptized in his name. The God of heaven signed and sealed his covenant with you! You have been at his holy table; again, and again he has signed and sealed his covenant with you. Stir up yourself and put on the armor of God. Follow the Captain of your salvation and fight against your flesh, the world, and the devil, according to your sacramental engagement! Show that it is to you a covenant of salt and not of snow, an unbreakable bond rather than a rope of sand!

Again, we must humbly plead his promises on our own behalf. Under oppression by any evil, or deprivation of any good, we may and ought to plead in prayer before him. Ministers often urge Christians to plead the promises. I wish that we all would plead the same as signed and sealed. God did not promise anything that he did not sign and seal in baptism and in the holy supper. So, go, distressed Christian, and fill your mouth with the promises of the Covenant of Grace. Plead your cause at the throne of grace.

Think this way, "Father, who cannot lie, you have sworn to me in the gospel that I shall have grace, glory, and no good thing withheld from me. You signed and sealed your promises to me in my baptism and have so done again and again as I partake of your supper. I have waited, do wait, and will continue to wait to my last breath through your grace, for you to perform what you have promised, sworn, and engaged under sign and seal."

This is how I mortify corruptions, repel temptations, quicken graces, revive hopes, attain joys unspeakable and full of glory. O that our best pulpits were less silent, and our best pews less ignorant, of the practical use of holy sacraments!

Part 3:
Truths on Assurance of Salvation

Question 3: What is that change brought about in a man by God's Holy Word and Spirit, before he can safely conclude himself to be passed from death to life?

"By one man sin entered into the world, and death by sin," (Rom. 5:12). Satan was a murderer from the beginning. He slew Adam by the first sin and slew all mankind in that first Adam. Spiritually speaking, we are all born dead. Dead in sin and dead for it. We are all dead in respect to corruption and dead in respect to condemnation. We are automatically condemned to the prison of hell and the torment of fire for the duration of eternity.

But, "God so loved the world, that he gave his only begotten Son," to redeem us from so great a death (John 3:16). God desires that we escape this eternal death through Jesus Christ, the way he provided for us to pass from death to life. And he urges us to come to this salvation through Christ.

If you ask, by what steps can we do this? I will answer, namely, by conviction, by humiliation, and by union to Christ. If you follow these steps as God designed, you can be assured of everlasting life.

Indeed, without divine intervention no man can take these steps. Creatures have no power but what is given them from God. Fallen man lacks the ability to be brought to grace and reconciliation to God on his own (Rom. 5:6).

Knowledge, will, and power necessary for salvation are all gifts of God, along with the purchase price of his Son's blood and his Holy Spirit who constantly works through the holy Word. Christ himself gained victory over Satan using the Word of God, and the Spirit will not, without it, work our victory over him (Matt. 4).

It is both possible, and necessary, that all who receive Christ as Savior and Lord live with assurance of salvation, because this same Word affirms it (2 Peter 1:10). Doubting salvation is the effect of sin. God does not ordinarily, if ever, withhold assurance from his children. But when Christians indulge themselves in their own lusts and omit their Christian duties, then to be sure, uncertainty is then itself a sin because it is produced by sin. Our eyes are blind if we cannot see how doubt is a result of sin. And that heart is hard indeed that does not treat doubt as both a cause and an effect of sin.

To be sure, all assurance attainable on earth is imperfect. But that which is attainable is true, proper, and powerful. True and proper because it is built on eternally true foundations. Powerful, as it produces peace and joy in ourselves and holiness and thanksgiving to God.

Nevertheless, it is a long while before most of God's children know their Father and grow beyond a point of doubting their salvation. In the initial stages of the conversion of the Gentile world to Christ, it was not so. The Holy Spirit's work of grace was more obvious then. And if you go back further to the old English puritans, they had more assurance among them than is seen in our day. They did not need our light as much as we need their heat. An unfamiliarity with the Covenant of Grace breeds unfounded hopes and unreasonable fears. With some of our people, every shadow of turning is recorded as a substantial conversion. And with others, that which is a right substantial conversion is only accounted as a shadow of turning from death to life.

With fear and trembling I will therefore attempt to resolve this question. Plainly, that I may be understood. Briefly, that I may be remembered. And fully, that my end may be attained – to make sinners ashamed of their peace and good men ashamed of their trouble. If my method is new, my doctrine is not. I go forward, praying that my efforts here are made successful by his Holy Spirit.

The change we seek has five components: spirit, covenant, qualities, conversation, and company.

Component 1. Of spirit. Man is an embodied spirit. His body is indwelt and actuated by his spirit. His spirit, though it is a free agent, is influenced by another spirit. In our created state, the Holy Spirit was in us and swayed us. Now, in our corrupted state, it is the spirit of Satan that is in us and leads us. It is certain, that as a result of the first transgression we forfeited the Holy Spirit's presence and influence and were given over to the influence of Satan, who is now called the, "god of this world," (1 John 4:4), and, "the prince that works in the children of disobedience," (Eph. 2:3). But in our renewed state there is a change of the actuating spirit. Satan is dethroned and cast out (Acts 26:18, 2 Tim. 2:26) when the Holy Spirit is given to us, poured into us, comes on us, rests on us, and leads us. He lives in the believer (1 John 4:4) so that the power of God can be great in them and victorious over the assaulting impure spirit.

Does one who is passed from death to life look different from the one who is not? No, because these spirits are invisible; therefore, the change is hardly discernable. Let these plain things be considered. These two spirits are infinitely dissimilar. They are both very active. Satan always works to the full extent of his power; the Holy Spirit works according to his will and pleasure. But both do work continually and strongly.

Though their natures are invisible, their operations are obvious. Satan leads one to evil; the Holy Spirit leads one to good. Ultimately, Satan turns away souls from Jesus Christ, his person, and his gospel. And ultimately, the Holy Spirit carries souls to the study and acceptance of both. His great work is to show Christ to us (John 16:14). His first work is to convince principally of the sin of unbelief in Christ. (And if this were the only sin, the sin of unbelief, it keeps men in all sin.) He works also to convince us of the righteousness of Christ, its perfection, its application to us, and its approval by God as the only righteousness that is acceptable to him. His Spirit also works to convince us of the conquest of Christ over all his and our enemies having both subjugated Satan and satisfied God (John 16:9-11). Having united us to Christ, he activates us for him (Rom. 8).

To conclude this, let the inquiring Christian argue that *Christ is mine, before life is mine!* Christ and his Spirit are always given together. Think to yourself, "If his Holy

Spirit is put into me, Satan is unseated. The Holy Spirit and the unclean cannot reign together. By the temper of my heart and ways, toward Christ especially, it is not hard to know whether he is expelled or still holds the throne in my soul. These I will diligently watch and examine whose superscription they bear – whether it is the Holy Advocate's or the enemy's. Enemies lead to death, advocates to life. By my guide, I will judge my way and end. And him I will count to be my guide whom I ordinarily and most desirously follow, whether it is the Holy Spirit or the contrary spirit."

And think also, "If I find that it is only on those occasions when terrors force it that I rely on the Holy Spirit and shun Satan's temptations, and that otherwise I deliberately and freely choose to embrace evil and reject holiness, that I rather Satan lead me in a sensually pleasurable life than the Holy Spirit direct me toward spiritual evangelism, then I will tell my soul that it is clear that all that is within me is as John 5:42 states, "I know you, that you do not have the love of God in you." On the contrary, if I find and discern that though I have been a cage to the most unclean bird, yet I am by grace turned into a temple of the Holy Spirit, and the very self-same spirit that dwelt in Christ dwells in me. Though I know little, he is daily teaching me; as forgetful as I am, he daily brings peace to my remembrance; as dull as I am, he daily by one thought or other encourages me to my duty so that I dare not omit it; as sad and sour as I am, every day he sweetens some promise of God to me; as often as I am out of frame for communion with God, and that is too often, he does not let me alone until I am restored. If this is what I find on examination of my heart and life, I will conclude there can only be life where there is such a spirit. And there can only be the best spirit where there are such operations. Hereby we know that he abides in us, by the Spirit that he has given us (1 John 3:24)."

Component 2. Of covenant. God delighted to deal with man by way of covenant. He bound the first man he made, and all his posterity, under the first covenant, the Covenant of Works. This covenant contained rich and honorable promises to us while requiring just and good demands from us. But man fell. He willfully broke this Covenant of Works, and by the fall so broke himself that he was never again able to do anything pleasing to God apart from the renewing grace of God. But this grace God only makes available under a new covenant. Anything man receives from God, he obtains through a new covenant relationship with this covenant-making God. Those that choose to hang onto the old Covenant of Works, doing all they do with design and hope to be forgiven for the sake and merit of it, the gospel declares their mistake to be mortal. Those who are under the works of the law are under the curse. That is, those who expect life and salvation as a reward for their own works of the law are under God's curse (Gal. 3:10). On the other hand, those who enter the new gospel covenant, the marriage covenant with Christ, are the only creatures who can bring forth fruit worthy of repentance. These have the Spirit of life, peace, and holiness abiding in them (Rom. 7:4).

Surely, God will never sign anyone's pass to heaven who never made his covenant a matter of their thoughts. A serious, seeking heart cannot help but ask, "Where do I stand with God?" You must continue this thought in this way, "As a creature, I can deserve no reward, no matter what I do! And why should I expect any? If I was bound by covenant without my knowledge in my original parents, does it not now concern me to get informed regarding the terms of that covenant? Covenants bind mutually; and if I do not know the terms, I cannot effect its use. If it is good for me, I cannot improve it, and if by any means it can be destructive, I am not capable of preventing it."

Then think, "So, if the sovereign Lord offers to take me into a better covenant, shall I not be concerned above all things in this world to learn its terms? At the same time, the greatest study of the covenant of grace, without profound thankfulness and hearty consent to it, only leads to man's condemnation! Knowledge of that covenant without consent is the most frightful symptom I know of a reprobate."

Indeed, there are only two covenants: a Covenant of Works and a Covenant of Grace that deal directly with men. These are vastly different. And so are the states of men who fall under the one and the other. Think to yourself, "My hopes shall die if I judge myself to be under the Covenant of Works, and my fears shall die if I judge myself to be under the Covenant of Grace. For if I am under the Covenant of Works, I am bound to a dutiful performance that is impossible for me to uphold for it requires perfect and perpetual obedience. Consequently, if I am under this covenant, I am under its curse as well (Gal. 3:10-11), and that curse is intolerable (Gen. 2:17). Not only that, if I am under this works-covenant, I have no mediator between God and me. I must go to prison because I cannot pay the price necessary to satisfy my sin debt. This Covenant of Works does not allow Christ, or any other advocate, to intercede for me before the offended Father. If I am under this covenant, it does not matter if I shed a sea of bloody tears for the least of my sins, it is still as unpardonable as the very sin against the Holy Spirit. And not only my sin, but my service as well, would be utterly contaminated."

Then consider, "And all of this justly too. Because if I abide under this covenant, it is due to my ignorance, my pride, and my enmity to God and Christ that I do so (Rom. 10:3). I am taught better, for in the gospel the righteousness of God is revealed. I am offered better, for the gospel invites me to the covenant of grace. So if I choose to remain under the deadly covenant, it is by my own desire (Gal. 4:21)."

The fruits of being under the Covenant of Works are plainly these: 1) Bondage and fear in one's spirit and efforts to keep out the love of God and the very desire to love him. 2) Great attention and care to things of the world and none, or next to none, to the purity of the inner man and the intentions of the heart. 3) Lack of dependency on Jesus Christ in things pertaining to God for assistance by his Spirit and acceptance through his blood. 4) Servility and a souring and embittering attitude toward all duty. 5) Rendering religion to being a task and a burden.

On the other hand, think to yourself, "I am not under the law but under grace if God has made this Covenant of Grace with me. If so, then the blessing of Abraham is upon me (Gal. 3:14). Reconciliation, justification, and adoption are my own. I partake in all the blessings of this covenant, and I am bound by all its duties. I am reconciled to God and he has promised to work all his perfections for my good. I will be to them a God," he says (Heb. 8:10). Jointly all, and distinctly, each of the three divine persons, have thus engaged. "Pardoning and purifying grace are expressly given to me, as is the crown of glory (2 Tim. 4:8)."

The fruits of souls that have chosen the better covenant are these. 1) They remember their slavery. They remember that they were Adam's children as soon as their souls and bodies were united in the womb. No sooner were they Adam's children, but they were also under Adam's covenant. And no sooner under his covenant but under his curse too. 2) Their eye and their heart are now upon the Father who said to his Son and Spirit, "Come, let us redeem man!" And upon the Son that said, "Lo, I come to do thy will!" Now God looks on this poor soul not as the first, but as the second Adam's child. 3) They joy in the Lord and rejoice in the God of their salvation. Their highest ambition is to rejoice in Christ Jesus and glory in him. 4) They love God's law and trust his Son. They love his law, have respect for every command, strive after perfection, and abound in all duty. But they do not trust in any works of their own. Having done all, they cry for Christ's Spirit for strength. Having done all, they cry for Christ's blood to make it acceptable. 5) They still know themselves to be unprofitable servants. If this is your state, then return to your rest, for the Lord has dealt bountifully with you! Meditate on this scripture, "all the paths of the Lord are mercy and truth to such as keep his covenant," (Psa. 25).

Component 3. Of qualities. If the spirit is changed, the covenant must necessarily be changed; and if the covenant is changed, the qualities of a man must also be changed. These are mysterious things and as a result, men attempt to explain them. But they are most, if not only, made known by their effects. We should think of them as the springs, seeds, and roots of our thoughts, words, and works and the evidences by which we are therefore determined to be holy or sinful. They are the treasures that are in a soul. Every man has an abundance of moral qualities; and all are dear to him, precious in his eyes. And depending on whether this treasure is good or evil, our Savior identifies the man to be good or evil (Matt. 12:35).

In the initial creation, the qualities of man were surely good because God endued our natural powers with all good qualifications. Qualities and dispositions for prompt and constant duty were planted in our mind. Our various powers and faculties depend much on each other for action. The practical depends on the affective powers, and they on the intellectual ones. But all were made upright, that is, with springs of goodness in them, apt to move as they ought towards each other within, and toward objects without (Eccl. 7:29).

But the first sin broke those springs, expelling those good qualities and introducing contrary ones. Since that point, man is capable of both holy qualities and sinful ones. The sin that drove out the first therefore, could not but bring in the latter, establishing springs of evil in us (Gen. 6:5, Rom. 8:7). Fallen man is compared to a disordered clock that strikes false every minute and does not have even one true motion before the maker mends it. How can a holy God delight in a creature in this way qualified – one that is disposed to no real good but to all evil, and that continually? If God involves himself in such work, he makes them into new creations. He recreates them into instruments that move with new springs. The old qualities are removed, and all becomes new. The evil treasure must be taken out, though it is bound up in the heart, and a good treasure must be laid in and alike bound up. Holy qualities must be infused.

Accordingly, we find everywhere in Scripture where God denounces wrath against all men of unrenewed natures. On the other hand, God reconciles those to himself who have put off the old man, crucifying the flesh with its affections and lusts. All such scriptural phrases express those who are born anew as parting with their inward roots of sin, their wicked dispositions, and their inclinations to evil.

They are likewise said to "put on the new man," and to be born again from heaven. They are pronounced to be men of another heart and spirit, "new creatures." That is, they are now of dispositions quite contrary to what they were before, inclined now to things that please God, whereas before they were inclined to things offending him.

It does not need to be said how hard it is to part from old qualities. Things glued together typically do not come apart without tearing. And until a heart is rent, there is no coming apart from its lust. But the necessity of the separation is clear, for God hates sin in his very nature, and even gospel grace cannot destroy his eternal nature. It implies the greatest of contradictions, that he who is holiness should cease to hate men who are bent toward ungodliness. And it is the darkest blasphemy for any to say that Christ came to save us in our sinful qualities and not *from* them.

A wise man would therefore know his qualities before judging his condition toward God. Those qualities that are predominant and reign in him determines the judgment of God on him. It is true that contrary qualities may dwell together in the same heart in low degrees; but in high degrees they cannot. Grace and lust are both found in even the best of souls. But they can no more reign together than water can boil and freeze together. So, my inquiry must be, what are those qualities that reign in me? What qualities sway my understanding, my affections, and my powers? The sinful qualities that bend all these to evil are the corruption of nature and original sin. The holy ones that bend all these to good are grace and the new nature within. Whichever of them prevails in me is the answer to my question.

Commonly, and I think justly, we consider four properties of a quality or disposition, namely, its causing to act readily without question, pleasantly without disgust, universally without exclusion, and constantly without intermissions. Now if original sin carries me into actual sin, I am far from the kingdom of God! If grace carries me to gracious actions, the kingdom of God is within me. To be a little more particular, there are three principles and eight instruments of holy qualities. The former are faith, hope and love. The latter are prudence, justice, temperance, courage, sincerity, humility, zeal, and constancy. Whether these, or the contraries of these, move me should be easy enough to discover from inward feelings and outward fruit.

But I am aware that mixtures of each obscure things. And in whom are not mixtures found? It is greatness that makes conspicuous. And where grace's victory is little, that is, next to none, I must not wonder at it. Rather I must labor to grow in grace and work to increase my spark to a flame.

Heaven and hell are inexpressibly different states. And I must believe that God will have those whom he places in the one and the other to be very differently qualified creatures. I must see that I have the principle, and then the proficiency of grace. Without the principle I have no qualification for heaven. And without the proficiency, I shall ever doubt the truth of my principle.

Component 4. Of conversation. A good spirit joins into a good covenant and infuses good qualities. But does he then leave them idle and dormant? No, for the end of all being is action. Besides, man is a creature that cannot be inactive. Grace leads him to act well; corruption, to act ill; but his very nature is to act much. Man exercises his powers and exerts his holy qualities toward God, towards himself, toward the angels above him, and toward those creatures around him congruously and harmoniously. Fallen man's thoughts and actions toward all is seen in the world as it is read about in the Bible. What is said of his thoughts may be said of his outward deeds. They are evil, only evil, continually toward God. Towards himself, they are idolatrous; towards his superiors, envious; towards inferiors, contemptuous; towards equals, jealous. Renewed man has quite a different attitude and behavior pattern toward all these mentioned. They walk, "after the Spirit," that is, according to the will and motion of the Holy Spirit, the Worker of grace, and according to the gracious quality and nature of his working in them. This is necessary for instruction, as God commands it. It is necessary for demonstrating God's glory. It is necessary for the edification of the church. It is essential for their Christian walk. For though we cannot merit our salvation by our works, this is the means by which a child of God lives his salvation out to the world.

    A necessity of design is present here also, as, "walking after the Spirit" is God's end in electing, redeeming, and calling men to himself. There is also a necessity of nature, for clean fountains send forth clean waters naturally, just as corrupt ones naturally produce the contrary. Finally, there is a necessity of covenant, for the covenant binds all who are his to ensure their daily walk, manner, attitudes, thoughts, and behaviors are consistent with those which honor and represent the gospel.

Woe to the vain men who cry for God's mercy while reproaching Christ's merits or undervaluing holy faith and good works. We must give each its proper place, or heaven will never be our place. He that thinks well and listens to God's Word, believing that God will not deny himself or alter his decrees, repeal his laws, or change his gospel to serve the preferences of a sluggard, he must conclude the same.

We all must remind ourselves that hope of reconciliation to God is essential to experiencing peace in this life. But holy living is also necessary to that hope. God did not promise to give his peace to those who live contrary to his truths and his Word.

Eternal thanks be to him for his new covenant, which is far short of legal perfection. Unallowed sins, and sins of mere infirmity, do not destroy peace with God. Willful sins cannot raise a storm that Christ's grace cannot cover for those who are truly penitent, desirous that they never again offend their God. I can only expect him to say to me, "Well done, good and faithful servant," if indeed by the gospel standard I have done well. At the same time, I believe God will say to me at judgment day, "depart, thou cursed," unless I live honorable to him and his covenant of grace.

But if my life reflects his truth, I can expect to hear him say, "Behold you damned angels and men whom I have forever abandoned! You have no cause to see me as unfair by setting this poor creature at my right hand. True, his sins were not few or small. Nor were his obediences great. But even if they had they been perfect, they could not have satisfied me for one sin, so they certainly cannot satisfy me, being short of perfect. My satisfaction and merit for their salvation is attained from another – my Son and their Savior. At the same time, I consider his good works sufficient to distinguish him from you and to stop your mouths by them. For you see, he obeyed my precepts, used my appointed means of life, answered my end in creation, walked according to the new nature I gave him, and persevered sincerely in the covenant I signed and sealed with him in my holy sacraments."

"To him that orders aright his conversation will I show the salvation of the Lord," (Psa. 50:23). "If we say that we have fellowship with him, and walk in darkness, we lie (*i.e. our walk contradicts our words*) and do not the truth," (1 John 1:6). "God will render to every man according to his deeds: to them who by patient continuance in well doing seek for glory and honor and immortality, eternal life. But to them who are contentious, and do not obey the truth, but obey unrighteousness, indignation and wrath, tribulation and anguish [*will come*] upon every soul of man that doeth evil..." (Rom. 2:6-9). "Who is a wise man, and endued with knowledge among you? Let him show out of a good conversation his works with meekness of wisdom," (James 3:13).

Component 5. Of company. God made us to crave company as much as we crave being itself. Being alone is almost the same as not being at all. Our souls need to be with others to feel complete. In addition, corrupt nature craves corrupt company, and sanctified nature craves sanctified company.

It is no wonder that the company we keep is so influential on us. Bad men are bettered by good; good men are worsened by evil. It is true that while we are in the world, we cannot avoid all bad company. But we also choose our company, and if we choose well the benefit is most wondrous. "He that walks with wise men shall be wise..." (Prov. 13:20). Also, the Holy Spirit calls in question the best saint's sincerity if he chooses to associate with wicked men (Job 34:8).

Everywhere in the Word we are told that love of the godly is the mark of one's love of God. And they that fear God's name love God's children and hate with a perfect hatred the infectious company of sinful men.

And who would not want to know himself by the same mark by which other men know him? In this way we may judge ourselves plainly. For if my company of choice does not change after my professed conversion to Christ, my attitudes and behaviors will also not change. Rather than changing from walking with men to walking with God, I would only be changing from one way of sinning to another. My inner qualities may only, in this case, be covered but not changed. One may then conclude that my supposed change of covenant was nothing more than a vain surmise.

"Come therefore, my soul, and let us reason together," to judge whether our calling and election of God are sure. Think to yourself, "What company I do keep of my own choosing? Prophane men are open graves, and hypocrites are painted ones. If I delight in graves and choose to keep my company among the dead, then it is certain that I will be buried with them forever."

Then consider, "Christ, on the other hand, is a tree of life that brings peace with God, holiness toward him, hope from him, glory with him. Saints only have life from Christ and, for this reason, are the only men on earth that are truly alive. If the Spirit that quickens me, the covenant that binds me, the qualities that possess me, and the way of life that employs me all find me among the living, then I am their companion in the kingdom of grace and shall surely be the same in his glorious kingdom."

And, "Therefore, before I can truly conclude the place of my eternal abode, I must consider the company I keep. Am I comfortable in the company of evil, as Sodom was? Do I have fellowship with God's enemies, or do I reprove them? Do I make a difference between sinful men and my Christian brethren? Do I hesitate to open the doors of my house and heart to ill men, lest the prince of darkness enter in and the prince of glory be shut out? Does my heart warm with joy when I see the pure in heart, those who love God? Do I salute each of them as David did Abigail? "Blessed be the Lord God of Israel which sent thee this day to meet me!" Finally, do I love those who love God, and hate them that hate him? And do these words of God dwell in me richly and powerfully, "O Lord, who may abide in Your tent? Who may dwell on Your holy hill? He who walks with integrity and works righteousness and speaks truth in his heart. He does not slander with his tongue, nor does evil to his neighbor, nor takes up a reproach against his friend. In whose eyes a reprobate is despised, but who honors those who fear the Lord," (Psa. 15:1-4). "They that fear thee, O Lord, will be glad when they see me (*i.e. a godly man*)," (Psa. 119:74). "He that walks with wise men shall be wise, but a companion of fools shall be destroyed," (Prov. 13:20).

Postscript

The desires of some, as well as the needs of others, invite me to place here this shorter answer to the third question.

The change in us after salvation is twofold; intellectual and practical. It effects our understandings and our conversations (*i.e. how we live*).

The intellectual change happens when these four points are learned and understood by us.

1. The principles of the doctrine of Christ are the foundations of Christianity. Who can trust in Christ as Savior and Lord who does not have at least a basic understanding of who that Christ is, the cornerstone of that spiritual building?

2. The conclusions that result from these principles are important. Building on the spiritual foundation is as necessary to the Christian life as the proper laying of the original foundation. There is no saving faith where the Holy Spirit is not teaching, and the soul is not learning to build up and build on in order to become a complete temple for the Holy Spirit (Eph. 4:12-15, 2 Peter 2:4-5).

3. There are confirmations of these same principles. The doctrines prove and strengthen the building, warranting our foundation and superstructure and securing them against winds of opposition. It is as needful to cover and preserve what we build from the injuries of weather, as it is to build in the first place, (Eph. 4:12, 16).

4. The applications of these afore-mentioned principles are equally important. The doctrines direct our growth and improvement to our Christian duties. Of what benefit are the means, but for the ends of them? What good do all God's truths do for our minds, if they do not improve us to all holy services in our lives? Who would build and protect a house and then not use it for themselves and their friends? The Spirit has not built and strengthened us in Christ for nothing. It is, rather, to teach us to make our life a service to him and to make his will, not our own, our law and rule for behavior toward God, ourselves, neighbors, friends, enemies, superiors, inferiors, and equals.

If you have truly passed from death to life, then you will know these things. Therefore, the ignorant, the apathetic, those who wish to remain embryos and dwarfs, or sand-builders at the mercy of the weather are not worthy to be called Christian.

The practical change has occurred when these four things can be said of a man.

1. He trembles at God's Word and desires to please him. He also gladly hears and receives the Word preached.

2. The change in him is as evident as the difference in a dark, cold, dead rock and a white-hot active fire. If he were ignorant before, he is now knowing. If lethargic before, he is now zealous for God in Christ. If industrious for the world before, he is now so for heaven.

3. He is changed into a man of God. That is, he is a man thoroughly furnished for every good work – for reading and hearing the Word profitably, benefitting from baptism

Postscript

and the Lord's Supper, submitting to church discipline, and governing his family rightly. By being furnished, he is also prepared with necessary skill and zeal.

4. He is changed from a deserter of the faith to a martyr. That is, he is resolved, by God's grace, to die the worst death rather than commit the least sin. He would rather be salted with fiery trials for the sake of the cross of Christ rather than burn in hell's fire.

FINIS

Other Helpful Works from Daniel Burgess at Puritan Publications

Directions for Daily Holy Living
by Daniel Burgess (1645-1713)

Holiness is not optional for the Christian. How should the Christian walk before God day after day? Burgess shows how Christians are to hear the word, pray, love their enemies, and take up all spiritual duties for the glory of God.

Foolish Talking and Jesting Described and Condemned
by Daniel Burgess (1645-1713)

This is one of those works that every Christian should read. In this work, Christians will have a difficult time dealing with its hard truths because every word, every thought, every time they "jest" in a manner not worthy of the Gospel, they bring reproach on God and Christ. This work challenges Christians to clean out their minds and mouths.

The Marks of a Godly Man
by Daniel Burgess (1645-1713)

Would other people say you are a heathen or a Christian? Daniel Burgess masterfully explains the difference between the heart of a wicked unconverted man and the heart of a truly changed man in Jesus Christ with the five marks of a godly man.

www.ingramcontent.com/pod-product-compliance
Lightning Source LLC
LaVergne TN
LVHW051528070426
835507LV00023B/3366